don't be shy,
dearest butterfly

Copyright © 2022 Libby Jenner

All Rights Reserved. No part of this book publication may be reproduced, stored in a retrieval system, or transmitted in any form by any means, electronic, mechanical, photocopying, recording, or otherwise, without the prior written permission of the author of this book. Except in the case of brief quotations embodied in reviews and certain other non-commercial uses permitted by copyright law.

Libby Jenner has the moral right to be identified as the author of this work in accordance with Copyright, Designs and Patents Act 1988.

Cover illustration by Annabelle Windsor

ISBN: 9798834545187
Imprint: Independently published

First printed in: United Kingdom
First Edition, 2022

@libbyjenner.poetry

don't be shy, dearest butterfly

BY LIBBY JENNER

Illustrated by Annabelle Windsor

A NOTE FROM THE AUTHOR

I hope that this book will bring comfort to you in moments of wilting and bolster you to bloom when you are ready to flourish. For me, and perhaps for you, healing is an ongoing process and sometimes we need to be encouraged to harness the fire that unchallenged pain has smothered or untangle our wings to soar into an ether of change.

The words embroidered into the pages of this book will remind you to nurture your inner child, and that they will thank you for the adoration you show yourself in all the versions of your divine being that you grow into.

Cocoons can keep you safe and offer you a place of rest when life seems too hectic to stand in the sun. But why don't you try something different? Don't be shy, dearest butterfly, and coax yourself out into the light.

Once you unfold your wings, you are limitless.

Libby

My poetry was birthed from a dark silence:
they rose from an ebony cocoon.
Though they may have been
conjured from an isolated pain
they loved the light of the moon.

My poetry wanted more of the light;
they now live under the
protection of the sun.
My poetry is lighter, despite what once was,
because, from harm, empowerment was spun.

PROLOGUE

don't be shy dearest butterfly

Libby Jenner

MY CANVAS

I have a canvas
I paint on it every day
normally it's colourful
recently it's grey

I'll try to reach for the yellow
a sun-kissed hue
I'll try to reach for another
perhaps deep ocean blue

or I'll try to get a forest green
but it's too far away
maybe I'll try for the whimsical purple
my mind is in disarray

I frantically grab a vermillion red
although it's normally quite a strain
but this red doesn't feel like love
it aches of trauma and pain

slowly, the life seeps from the paint
there's no alive colour left in it
yet I still stalk subconsciously to my canvas
inhibitions of a puppet

I cry at myself to push harder
to run to the other paints
but I'm lost in a trance and cannot be found
consumed by fear and hate

I know I want the other colours
it hurts to see them so close

don't be shy, dearest butterfly

all I want is a colourful canvas
but grey is what they chose

they know I can't cope with other colours
my identity is revolved around grey
who am I without this comfort?
if we lost control, I am to blame.

they won't pull me back to safety
if I try a new colour for my design
and with their voices echoing so loud
it is difficult to even hear mine

I went to my canvas again, today,
but I had something hidden.
For underneath my protective cloak
rested a colour that was forbidden.

Before they noticed, I chucked the paint:
it streamed right over the sides.
They screamed and howled, but I couldn't hear:
their game I would no longer abide.

But the colour is not what you would guess;
it wasn't extravagant, but bright.

I smiled in relief at *my* fresh start:
a canvas of pearly white.

Libby Jenner

don't be shy, dearest butterfly

PROTECTED BY
THE LIGHT OF THE SUN

Libby Jenner

don't be shy, dearest butterfly

I stood in front of a fresh pearl canvas, white caramel oozing over the edges, still. Pots of grey paint were lined intricately on a small table in the far corner of a featureless room. I grabbed at my jacket to check my notebook was still inside, and I sighed in relief as I felt the hardcover under the soft material of my pocket.

All at once, beams of light trickled over my vision. I squinted as a wooden door, that seemed to have appeared out of nowhere, was opened cautiously and a silhouette beckoned me towards them. There was an air of comfort about their presence.

I opened my mouth but before I could speak, the sun kissed shadow said, "Hey, I am your guide. Would you like to take a walk with me?"

I followed them into a celestial-like garden, and the sweet rose aroma was blissfully intoxicating with my first breath out of the door. Fiery foliage with a crimson blush adorned leafy bushes. The cerulean sky was painted with neat brushstrokes of pink sand clouds. Orange blossoms swayed in a citrus breeze of sweet beginnings whilst golden blades of dappled light pierced through the canopy of leaves:

illuminating the dewy grass below. I couldn't help but caress the ivory lace petals of the flowers at my feet: their cedar centres glittered with pollen that the humble bees flying above me were eager to sprinkle themselves with.

Within walking distance was a quaint home with delicate yellow gardenia walls: flowers weaved themselves in vines around the golden oak front door and forget-me-nots dotted themselves along the base of the walls. Large bay windowsills housed a balayage of woodland green potted plants, and one grew so tall it almost reached the roof: a roof sewn together by ribbons of ivy. Attached to the side of the right wall was a spacious greenhouse which, upon further inspection, accommodated a colourful community of butterflies amongst colossal leafy plants.

"Are you not curious?" they asked me, gently. I turned in surprise to acknowledge the woman who had led me out of the door. But I had no words, so I fumbled with the bottom of my top and stared at my feet that were planted firmly on the grass. "Perhaps you would like to take a walk? Are you ready?" she

don't be shy, dearest butterfly

enquired with soothing tones. I gazed in awe at the beauty around me; I felt comfortable, safe, and secure. As if seeing the hesitation in my demeanor, she said to me softly, "You will come back here, I promise, we can walk through the meadow as you like the flowers so much?" I nodded, at her. And she offered her hand to me. "Okay then, my little sunflower, let's get going."

The guide led me to a meadow of heavenly colours just on the outskirts of an open forest. "Would you like to pick some flowers? How about some yellow ones? I'll wait just here for you."

I thanked her as she passed me a wicker basket to collect my flowers in and I walked away smiling, because yellow is my favourite colour.

I walked towards a patch of buttercups and knelt on the sun-soaked earth. I twirled a stem around in my fingers and I remembered something from the lemon hue: a memory of holding buttercups under the chins of my friends to see how much they loved butter. I picked up my wicker basket of buttercups, glanced

Libby Jenner

briefly at my guide, who nodded with a smile, and I ran into the canopy of trees.

I laughed in excitement and twirled in circles as tendrils of my hair danced with the breeze. I plucked myself some scarlet roses, decorated in my basket with blushing primroses. I then found some periwinkle petals to complement my collection and lilac florals for my bouquet creation.

"How much do I love myself?" I asked out loud, as I held a buttercup under my chin. A rainbow luminescence enshrouded my body, it seems the adoration I had was divine.

The guide, who had followed not far behind, said as a spoken thought, "How funny, we always asked if we loved butter, when a different question could have made so much more light shine."

"Why did you call me a sunflower?" I asked her, as we walked further into the sage crown of trees, "You didn't even ask for my name?"

The guide beckoned me to a mossy tree stump, which we perched on, as she began replying to my question.

"You are right, I didn't ask for your name, but there is

don't be shy, dearest butterfly

something familiar in you that reminds me of a sunflower.

You see,

Your yellow hue
is as strong as your wit.
Your stem is tall
and helps you stand proud.
And you brighten any room
you are placed in.
So, please,
never undermine your power.
For your name is graced
by both the sun
and a flower.

"You are constantly growing and blooming, so is it not the truth that we are all, in our own uniqueness, much like a flower? But I guess flowers are also fragile, so it depends on how you perceive strength, too. What do you think?"
I sat in thought for a moment, and then picked up one of the red roses from the wicker basket.

Libby Jenner

Rose petals,
soft as a sunset
and fragile with beauty.

But try and pick one
with your bare hands.
you will weep
both tears and blood.

Rose thorns,
sharp as brisk winds,
and devious as ice.

One must not touch.
Just because there's beauty
doesn't mean
they won't bite.

A rose,
though pretty to look at,
will cut grabbing hands.

Think twice
before you touch us roses.
We are less fragile
than you deem.

If you harass the flowers,
pick at their roots,
you will start to hear
us scream.

don't be shy, dearest butterfly

"I think you can be both fragile and strong, assertive and vulnerable, or sensitive and confident. And they can work together and not against each other… but I'm not sure if that makes sense and I'm probably wrong and -"

The guide placed her hand on my shoulder to interrupt my trailing sentence, "I think that's a wonderful answer."

I could barely conceal the beaming blush that stretched across my face.

Libby Jenner

don't be shy, dearest butterfly

GUARDED BY
THE EYES OF THE MOON

Libby Jenner

don't be shy, dearest butterfly

Dusk had long been painted over by the ebony night sky; the fireflies had taken their permanent rest in its extensive darkness. The guide helped me start a small fire to sit around and warm up by before we journeyed back to the house: flames of sunbaked autumn whispered amongst themselves over the smoldering branches of wood. "I am just going to collect some firewood", the guide said, "I will be right back, I promise."

I was left to tend to our small fire, the flames were trying their hardest to keep dancing, but they began to grow tired. My eyes began to twitch with every shadow movement as I slowly became aware of the dark silence enveloping me.

The dark never scared me, really, I was more afraid of what lurked in the shadows than the shadows themselves. But the darkness around me seemed slightly suffocating. I could feel the garlands of night tighten around my throat. The dim light of our fire was slowly fading; their dance now awaiting an applause as the flames took their last bow.

My palms became damp, and my heart began thumping so hard against my ribs that the fear of my heart escaping from my chest amplified the concerns that were already manifesting in every part of my body. I steadied myself from the crumpled position I was sat in and gazed up at the moon's divine face for reassurance.

don't be shy, dearest butterfly

I groan as my neglected wings outstretch,
and I bask them in the moonlight's serenity.
"Please, waning moon, heed my call.
This lonely aviary has left me flightless,
my feathers are smothering my lungs,
and my wings crave restoration.

I don't want to fall, anymore.

Please radiate your energy of healing,
let it coat my frail throat that beckons you,
and guide me to my freedom key.
Can you hear me? Please do!
I will now stop my worried pleads
and listen out for you."

The wind caressed my shivering skin with soft words
that were passed down from the moon above.

My wings awoke to the sound of her lullabies,
outstretched as if awaiting an embrace.
And I exhaled the negative energy
after every cleansing breath,
as the moon had instructed
in their whispered breezes.

"I am forever in awe
of your bolstering vision.
Thank you for reminding me
of my love and light.
Your divine benevolence
has set me free."

Libby Jenner

When the guide returned, the fire was burning so bright and with so much ferocious potential that she could do nothing but hang her mouth open and laugh in awe.

"And how did you manage to do that? This is phenomenal!" she exclaimed with so much delight I thought she was going to start dancing on the spot but couldn't because of the wood balancing in her arms. I giggled with her as she placed down the jobless branches, and we jumped around the waltzing fire until our legs were so tired that we collapsed in a frenzied heap on the woodland floor.

I scuffed the leaves on the path as we walked in the indigo infused woods back to the soft lights of the house, my hands firmly in my pockets and fingers picking at the loose threads in the stitched-pocket lining. "Guide… if that's what I call you… how do I know I can always pull myself out of the darkness? What if I get so consumed by it that I end up back in a sort of… emotional abyss? What if there isn't always light from the sun or the moon to help me and what if…"

don't be shy, dearest butterfly

She placed her hand on my shoulder attentively: instantly soothing my worried state with her reassuring touch. "Well…" she began, "there is no saying whether you will or won't. But becoming comfortable with uncertainty, though as difficult as this can be, and reassuring yourself that you have experienced good moments before, and so they are likely to happen again, may help? And even if you did, end up in a bad mindset, your hopes and dreams were spun amongst calamities that you experienced and there is strength in that, don't you see? When you could have chosen cataclysmic destruction, you invoked healing means.

"You have survived so many torments already, yet you are still brimming with passion. So be proud of yourself for the moments of happiness that you draw into your life. Bad days may come, but I think you know already what you would do if they did: you've fought inner battles before, your victories have only just begun."

I sat there for a moment to allow her calm words to swim to my rapid thoughts. "So…" I began, "what if... I like the darkness? What if I was in the abyss for so long that I didn't want to come out?"

She turned to face me, her misty blue eyes full of inquisition, and said, "You can seek comfort in the darkness, you might unearth some emotions that need to be addressed, but you are then neglecting all the light in the stars around you! Would you not miss feeling the sun soak into your skin? Or miss the musical light of the moon as she sings to the universe?

"Darkness can only keep you company for so long before it swallows you; that is when you must try your best to muster your energy, place your ladder, and climb out."

By the time we reached the door of the house, I was almost falling asleep whilst standing. The guide led me up a small spiral set of stairs and into a spacious room. I walked straight to the bed and sunk into its warm embrace. "Sleep well, I will see you in the morning," whispered the guide. Through my dozing eyes I saw her falter at the edge of the bed, but she shook her head, sighed slightly, and tiptoed out of the room.

That night was one of the best sleeps I had experienced in a very long time.

I woke up to the soft glow of sun dripping through ivory curtains. I rubbed my eyes and stared in bewilderment at the pretty room that I had been too tired to digest the night before.

The double bed had small bumblebees embroidered into the white duvet sheets and was centred against the back wall. I pulled myself off the side of the bed and planted my feet onto cool wooden floorboards. As I walked towards the curtains and pulled them open, I noticed a potted monstera in the corner of the room adjacent to a vintage looking bookcase overflowing with vibrantly bound books: some had been stacked in a neat pile to one side and were topped with a cactus. At the far end of the room was a large wooden wardrobe and chest of drawers which were full of clothes and trinkets.

I assumed this was the guide's room, and after realising she was most likely waiting for me to wake up I dashed down the sunflower carpeted stairs (stopping occasionally to admire the bright posters framed on the walls) and directed myself towards the faint sound of classical music emitting from what I soon found out to be the lounge.

I was so excited to see the guide and ask her all about the house, what we were going to do today, and whether I could borrow any of her books, but something wasn't quite right.

She was draped over a plush peacock armchair; one hand was tapping on the left side of it and the other hand cradled her forehead. At the sound of my footsteps, she must have awoken from her forlorn state. I'm not sure who she was trying to fool with her forced smile, as it certainly wasn't convincing me.

"How did you sleep?" she asked genuinely as she rose from her chair to turn off the radio.

"Oh fine…yeah… great actually… thank you!" I replied with as much enthusiasm as I could muster, but my eyes were fixated on the bulging rucksack next to the chair. She followed my eyeline to her packed bag, took a deep breath, and gestured for me to sit in the armchair. She pulled a stool from her desk

don't be shy, dearest butterfly

under the windowsill to sit opposite me. I took this moment to see that next to me was a small table with a bell-shaped lamp perching on it, but what caught my attention more was the pristine and untitled notebook next to it.

The guide picked the notebook up and placed it in my hands, "Take this book and write about the adventures you have exploring the forest and meadows. Write about what you learn, what challenges you face, and anything else that inspires you. You can stay here as much or as little as you like: there is no time limit to how much you visit here. It's a nice break from the outside world. I have certainly learnt that.

"I also have a handful of seeds for you to sprinkle as you explore, I thought you might enjoy reminiscing the moments you have here when the flowers bloom. I would love for you to have them," she said as she rummaged in her dungaree pockets for the seeds.

I didn't even try to hide my confusion, I had only just met her, and I had so many unanswered questions and I could feel all of them bubbling inside of me and attempting to erupt. "But… where are you going? I love it here but… what if something bad happens or I need help or…" I couldn't tell whether it was a tear in her eye or if her eyes shined brighter today than they had yesterday, but she embraced me in a hug that filled my entire body with tranquility. Her safety blanket arms were enough to alleviate the anxieties I had. "Why now? Why have you got to go?" I pleaded, my head still resting on her shoulders and arms looped around her waist. I could feel her hands softly stroking the roots of my hair.

"The door that you came through yesterday, one has appeared for me. And it feels right to walk through it, just like your door appeared when you were ready for something new. I know I need to go, I'm just sorry I didn't get a lot of time with you," she replied shakily.

I walked with her to the front door, and we had one last embrace. She whispered in my ear: "I may not be with you, but I hold you in my arms, always. Even when you can't feel it."

don't be shy, dearest butterfly

Libby Jenner

SEASONAL STORIES
(written in my notebook)

don't be shy, dearest butterfly

Libby Jenner

YEAR ONE

Spring Vision

Daffodils

Hello, spring flowers

Dots of Hope

Sundays are the epitome of soft

I am refusing to live with a fear of change

A kiss from Autumn feels like

Whispers

Spiralling

Dark nights

Snow drop in the city

Not quite ready

don't be shy, dearest butterfly

Libby Jenner

SPRING VISION

Dawn bloomed
in delicate pastel shades,
the colours floated through
my closed eyelids,
awakening me
from my comatose.

In my daze,
a realisation bled over me:
I had been away from the sun
and deprived myself of her company.
How had I survived so long
without her loving gaze?
Would she still let me bask
in her brilliance
after my absence?

I turned the dusty door handle
and pushed open my front door.
To my delight,
she let me ease myself into
her silky peach sorbet glow.

My breathing became lighter,
my thoughts so much brighter,
and in that moment, I was revived.

don't be shy, dearest butterfly

Libby Jenner

DAFFODILS

I sat on a pollen covered chair
hoping
that the bees will help grow
the patch of wilted daffodils
at my side.

But
maybe,
I am the wildflower,
that the daffodils are mirroring,
who is in desperate need
of a reprise?

don't be shy, dearest butterfly

Libby Jenner

HELLO, SPRING FLOWERS

How sweet, you are,
to let the bees rest
in your powdered beds.

It is always a delight
when I first hear the buzz of the bee:
it is how I know spring is near.

I love how the lilac
and pearl snowdrops
cosy themselves
at the base of tree trunks.

And the teetering tulips,
that have their delicate leaves
gemmed with dew,
are so deliciously vibrant.

The earth under my feet
feels softer,
nurtured:
petrichor is a delight for you all,
I'm sure.

I await in excitement
for what your blooming
awakens.

don't be shy, dearest butterfly

Libby Jenner

DOTS OF HOPE

Forget-me-nots weave amongst the grass
along the base of my house:
their cerulean petals,
and sunshine centres,
gaze up at me as I enter and leave my abode.

They are a reminder that,
though I may be feeling blue
on the outside,
there is a constant warmth
within me.

And it's best not to forget it, either.

don't be shy, dearest butterfly

Libby Jenner

SUNDAYS ARE THE EPITOME OF SOFT

Shell pink tulips yawning wide
in a pearl vase bed.
Open windows,
with the sun splintering through chiffon curtains,
and a dusty glow caressing the walls.
Painted birds symphonising
in warm, lyrical breezes.
A book nestled on my lap,
pages crinkled with sea salt,
and a chai in my hand
with clunking ice cubes.

In this moment, I wish to stay:
a soft summer Sunday.

don't be shy, dearest butterfly

Libby Jenner

I AM REFUSING TO LIVE WITH A FEAR OF CHANGE

I have sauntered past many bridges, lately:

arched	straight,
cobbled,	colossal,
descending	ascending.
moss engulfed	pristine stones,

But I feel like I cannot cross them.
I'm too scared of falling over the side.

But there are new kinds of light
over the bridges:
one has dusted dahlia moonbeams,
another has syrup glazed sunlight,
and I so frantically want to discover
what they expose.

So here I am,
at the edge of my current reality,
I have embroidered my fears into feathers
so even if this bridge surrenders beneath me
I can fly without fear.

don't be shy, dearest butterfly

Libby Jenner

A KISS FROM AUTUMN FEELS LIKE

The crisp gaze of morning illuminating crystal beads on spiderwebs / my heart beating in time with stardust fireworks / the aroma of a chai latte swirling around me as I bring a wide ceramic mug to my blushed lips / glass-like sheets of frost bound over grass / crunching fallen leaves beneath my feet that carpet the floor with terracotta, fawn, and mocha hues / amber lights draped along walls of a dusky room and pumpkin candles glowing in the corners/ sipping on the last drops of September to savor the taste of cinnamon-spice / earthy aromas lingering on your clothes after a downpour

don't be shy, dearest butterfly

Libby Jenner

WHISPERS

I whisper to the darkness
to tease my monsters,
I dance with fire
to entice my demons,
and I sing with storms
to drown them all.
Back into my head
they will no longer crawl.

Occasionally,
when I whisper seductive notes
to the darkness,
fewer monsters
snarl back.
And sometimes,
when I dance with fire,
fewer demons join me.
So, when I sing with storms,
there is nothing to drown:
I am left to swim in the tranquil sea.

But I won't stop whispering
or dancing.
Motivation, I must uphold:
I will continue to face my fears
until they are too scared to return,
and are merely fairy tales
to be unashamedly told.

don't be shy, dearest butterfly

Libby Jenner

SPIRALLING

I am in a house
with lots of stairs.
I start at the bottom
and realise
something is after me.

I run.

I try to find
a window
to escape
but someone lights a match,
the ground blows up
in snarling flames.

I drag my coughing body
through the smoke
and somehow stumble
across an exit.
All I must do now
is run,
again.

But now
there are people
c i r c l i n g.
I grab the nearest object,
a metal bar
on the floor,
and I swing.
It makes contact.
But they are

don't be shy, dearest butterfly

immortal.

They laugh at my horror
and then
they swing.

When I awake,
I am in a house
with lots of stairs.

The next time someone asks me:

"You were fine yesterday, what is so different today?"

I will tell them:

Some days finding the exit is easier, sometimes I find a stronger object to hit with, and sometimes the things that chase me don't seem so scary. But no matter what I do, I will awake and

I will be in a house
with lots of stairs.

And I don't know how to get out.

Libby Jenner

don't be shy, dearest butterfly

DARK NIGHTS

What I experience is valid,
it's time to unpack how I feel.
Because my body is signaling
what my mind is struggling to heal.

I will not apologise for
the vulnerability of my emotions
because I am learning to regulate myself
when my triggers are in motion.

This safe space I have conjured
is the start to my growth
and I am proud that I am prioritising
my wellbeing the most.

I understand, now,
that my feelings were never a weakness:
they show me what needs to be addressed.
And though my journey will differ each day,
all I can give is my current best.

Libby Jenner

don't be shy, dearest butterfly

SNOW DROP IN THE CITY

I am hungry
for sunlight.
My leaves stretch
in the darkness.
The soil is hard,
and dry.
The holes
in the top of the box
tease me,
I can't squeeze
beyond my constraints,
but four beams
of light
filter through.

s t r e t c h

not
quite
enough

s t r e t c h

almost
there

squeeze

a single leaf makes it through.
The sun gives me strength:
roots burst from the soil
puncturing the cardboard,
and my stem forces the lid off.

Libby Jenner

I breathe.

I thought getting out of the box
was the hardest part,
but now I stand as a lone flower,
still with buds to grow,
in the middle of a concrete city
with snow dusted floors.

don't be shy, dearest butterfly

Libby Jenner

NOT QUITE READY

Winter ran through the mist,
its icy kisses leaving red marks
on my fingertips.

I hurried through the forest to
get to the warmth of home
and escape the winds that,
through the skeletal trees, moaned.

When in my peripheral vision
I saw an envious blur,
I lingered for a moment
to try and observe.

On closer inspection,
it was a peridot-coloured door
with a twisted lever handle
of golden ore.

It was built into the trunk
of a swaying willow tree
and I reached for the handle,
curiosity took over me.

But the door wouldn't open,
no matter how much I tried,
and the racing winter was getting stronger
with every one of my reluctant sighs.

I don't think the door
was ready for me to open.

don't be shy, dearest butterfly

Or, at least,
that's what the icy winds
had spoken.

Libby Jenner

don't be shy, dearest butterfly

YEAR TWO

Blue is new

Learning to be gentle with my harsh thoughts

Change of address

This is not a sprint

A reminding letter

Blossom Tree

Whispered into the wind

In sickness and in health

Slipping on an icy step

The aftermath

Lessons of Love

Melting Modifications

Libby Jenner

don't be shy, dearest butterfly

BLUE IS NEW

There's something magical in the sky when spring has awakened.

As the end of daytime flirts with the beginning of night, and the moon is a pale etching, the sky blends into cornflower blue splendor.

Yet, out of all my favourite colours, I never considered blue to be one of them: the connotations of sadness and despair were a significant deterrent.

But this blue is nothing like its reputation depicts.

This blue speaks tales of lovers who stole kisses before dark, seas filled with enchanting creatures that tease humanity just below their surface, people waiting in anticipation for the moon to show and begin their transformation, and tales in the clouds from the souls that gaze down upon us.

And I'm left thinking, what else in the world have I ignored because of people's assumptions that have attached themselves to me?

In the future, I will think of this blue when I am around people with differing ideas. I will picture the small scratch of white paint in the cornflower canvas and remind myself that though I may be the only wolf staring at it in awe, I am content with who I want to be.

Libby Jenner

don't be shy, dearest butterfly

LEARNING TO BE GENTLE WITH MY HARSH THOUGHTS

Carmine roses threatening their thorns,
and wine stains at their roots,
but with the scintillating coating
of my dragon scale armour
bouquets of roses fill my rooms.

Whether it was my care of wearing
protection on my hands,
or the thoughtfulness of the roses
to hide their thorns from me,
I somehow managed to defy their harsh stems
and prove that I can be gentle with ferocity.

Libby Jenner

don't be shy, dearest butterfly

CHANGE OF ADDRESS

Letters of hatred can corrupt a heart:
it makes people scream shriller than a banshee.
But my heart delivers love in plenty,
because it is enveloped by poetry.

Libby Jenner

don't be shy, dearest butterfly

THIS IS NOT A SPRINT

I must remind myself to walk slower,
so that I can breathe in the present,
and see that life cradles a better narrative
than what the memories of an old home
wrote in blurred bruises across my body.

I must remind myself to walk slower,
so I may see the sky glistening with promise
and let the sun drip happiness over me
to quench my thirst for gratitude.

I want to walk slower,
so that my salted wounds turn sweet
and I am content with where it is
I am journeying to.

I am walking slower, now,
and when I have found my definition,
that the past has not grazed over my name,
I'll choose
to finally

stop.

Libby Jenner

don't be shy, dearest butterfly

A REMINDING LETTER

My summer warrior,

You are protected, not just for what you wear on your exterior, for you incessantly turn the wisps of your trauma into golden threads to sew yourself back together.

Each time, you heal stronger.

The faith in your success, the determination to become a greater version of yourself, and the love that you explore, I have witnessed your mind sew them all.

It's you.

YOU are the armour.

And, oh my,
you are indestructible.

Libby Jenner

don't be shy, dearest butterfly

BLOSSOM TREE

My book is open on my lap,
pages soft though crinkled with time,
as light filters through her delicate pink petals.
Shafts of gold illuminate the words
as she sways with a calming intonation.

Her trunk is strong behind my back
as I sit at her base.
I plant my sore feet in the cooling dew,
that coats the mahogany ground
around her strands of roots,
and let the grass weave between my toes.
Tendrils of aloe calmness curl around my ankles:
the feeling floods through my body
and oozes over my tense skin.
The earth diffuses its nurturing minerals into me
in waves of refreshing thoughts.

She, the blossom tree,
anchors me to the present.
And lets me know I am safe
because my foundations are, now,
in healthy soil.

Libby Jenner

don't be shy, dearest butterfly

WHISPERED INTO THE WIND

Breathe in.
Breathe out.
Untangle your fretful doubt.
Let the vermillion shades of autumn
brush flushes of motivation on your vision.
And allow the crisp breeze from icy clouds
to encourage the fleeing of indecisions.

Plumes of twilight
shall radiate saffron rays over your mind.
Your stifled light is free,
and your branches of hope
are becoming intertwined.

If now is not the time to care for yourself, when?

Better now before the frost kicks in,
and winter will be here,
again.

Libby Jenner

don't be shy, dearest butterfly

IN SICKNESS AND IN HEALTH

As the last lingering leaves of autumn
created a ripe grapefruit peel rug on the floor
I have realised that the shift of season
has enlightened me.

All the days I stayed indoors with a book,
all the nights I fed my body
with a home-cooked meal,
all the hours I danced in my room
and sung to my favourite playlist,
all the minutes I cried
as I collapsed with my emotions,
and all the seconds I devoted to my presence
made me feel more confident
and reassured with myself.

Whilst nurturing my mind and body
I have found,
I am rather good company.

(And I cannot believe I was made to feel otherwise)

Libby Jenner

don't be shy, dearest butterfly

SLIPPING ON AN ICY STEP

I am in D i S a R r A y:
emotions painted with a palette of
miscellaneous madness.
I scrape the colour with a knife
and it becomes my accessory to a crime
as I scratch it over the missing pages of this book
that I cut out and folded into my old notepad.

I wish I had the desire to burn them,
but b.l.o.t.t.i.n.g colour onto the dark pages
seems more… *expulsive.*
For now, they stay locked in my drawer.
Dust accumulating under the skin of words
that were too harsh for my gentle narrative:
a reminder that I am only human
and I am allowed to fall
so long as I learn how to stand, again.

Libby Jenner

don't be shy, dearest butterfly

THE AFTERMATH

Tendrils of thoughts pirouette around my room
as I try to sleep, in frustration.

Perhaps if I hadn't been overthinking for hours
I wouldn't remain in agonising contemplation,

Libby Jenner

don't be shy, dearest butterfly

LESSONS OF LOVE

Bitter memories frost-bound to me
form glaciers around my heart.
But my inner fires are thawing my thoughts
and the ice is falling apart.

Chilled to the bone I refuse to be:
no longer will winter be a host.
I am befriending the snowflakes,
to freeze this moment,
where I am choosing to love myself the most.

Libby Jenner

don't be shy, dearest butterfly

MELTING MODIFICATIONS

Being dressed up in snowflakes was fun,
for a time.

Wintry characters draped glistening icy robes over my shoulders, and frosted jewels encrusted my ears and wrists.

But they watched with glee as my delicate gown shattered in glass shards and melted beneath the warm sun.

I'd grab at the layers of water fabric, but I was left with nothing but angel tears in my hands: all that had fallen in a hot cascade across my red cheeks as my naked body trembled with every laugh.

This is a feeling I want to leave behind this year.
I am drained of being gifted with glass-bound promises tied in strings.

So, next year, I will thaw with the flowers, bloom among them, and leave the winter spirits alone.

Because it has taken me far too long to realise that I have been trying so hard to settle with the snow

when I am a daughter of spring.

Libby Jenner

don't be shy, dearest butterfly

YEAR THREE

Wilting

Walking in the spring ether

Garden gossip

Warm tones

The parts of nature I couldn't live without

Am I a poem?

Tempted but not fooled

A writer's life is my greatest gift

Cleanse

Weathered by change

Ice on wounds

Anarchic ambience

Libby Jenner

don't be shy, dearest butterfly

WILTING

My fragile stem cowers
before roseate palms,
and my bloss*change*oming
is obstructed by fear.

But my roots grow stronger
with every season,
so my emotional equinox
will be different this year.

I will unconditionally love my new bloomed self
more intense than I loved her before:
for every lifetime with a fresh version of me
shows more parts of myself to adore.

Libby Jenner

don't be shy, dearest butterfly

WALKING IN THE SPRING ETHER

You are a miracle forged from the sun and moon to shed light on the lives you touch.

Your capabilities are endless: bravery and vulnerability flow in your blood alongside the currents of confidence in your veins.

You are successful in any positive opportunity that your path guides you to; and you consistently absorb wisdom from the side-line difficulties.

You have a fire within you that is both ferocious and powerful; you can achieve anything you desire with those fearless flames.

Let no one distract you from your own happiness; when in episodes of doubt, remember that you are your safe space.

You are filled with an abundance of compassion that envelopes your words as you speak to yourself and others around you.

You are unstoppable, like an almighty lightning bolt with instructions to shatter the Earth's crust.

You are incredible. A being with no limits. To undermine your greatness, would be the ultimate bluff.

Libby Jenner

don't be shy, dearest butterfly

GARDEN GOSSIP

The sun's rays made me tired
so I rested my head amongst the flowers,
how kind that they grow where I once wilted,
and as I drifted into a daydream
I overheard them whisper:

"I told you she could do it.
Look at her!
No longer will she be hungry for light
when she glows the way she does, now."

Libby Jenner

don't be shy, dearest butterfly

WARM TONES

The summer daylight seeped
into the pores of my skin,
and the moon shone brighter
from the reflection of my beaming grin.

I twirled around under azure skies
as my hair danced with the breeze:
my feather footsteps synchronised
with the soft rhythm of the trees.

Caressed by success, my mind wanders
to my myriad of dreams and desires.
How proud I am, of myself,
that my growth has dispersed like wildfires.

Libby Jenner

don't be shy, dearest butterfly

THE PARTS OF NATURE I COULDN'T LIVE WITHOUT

Adopting the sun to wallow in its warm gaze and let her scare my shadows away / fresh affirmations to guide me into paths I can make peace with / the colours of the dawning day that embellish the sky with honey punch and mulberry rose gloss / long walks to find lakes of lilac silk water / perching amongst ferns and listening to enchanted stories that the trees whispered to them / inhaling scents of clementine and savoring their citrus taste / buttermilk petals being beds for fuzzy bees with pollen dusted tums / soft cotton snow on windowsills with robin prints dotted on the surface

Libby Jenner

don't be shy, dearest butterfly

AM I A POEM?

I am the orange glow
on the underbelly of lilac clouds
in no rush to heal overnight

my lilac side not pouring, yet,
but instead
content in moving
along the delicate silk of sky

am I a poem?
is all that I am moving towards
composed of words and scenic metaphors?

perhaps

how beautiful, that is

Libby Jenner

don't be shy, dearest butterfly

TEMPTED BUT NOT QUITE FOOLED

The sky was strung with fairy lights, tonight. I could see them shining down at me from my bedroom window. I drew a little heart in the condensation that the frost laced glass had acquired and placed my aching head against the coldness.

For a moment, I let the darkness creep into my skin; I welcomed their familiar feel with open arms.

Autumn's whispers grazed at the window, but I could barely make out their words. I was so lost in thought as I walked further and further into the sinister forest where shadows lurked, and silhouettes enticed me into their abyss.

I opened my eyes with a start. I thought the shadows had finally got me. But I looked down and noticed my own arms wrapped around myself.

She was right, I thought, as I gazed up at the twinkling sky. *I would miss the light of the stars if I let the darkness absorb me.*

And on that note, I grabbed a book to read in my plush chair, turned on the bell-shaped lamp, and let the delicate light enshroud me in safety.

The darkness may be an old friend, but old friends have been left behind for a reason.

Libby Jenner

don't be shy, dearest butterfly

A WRITER'S LIFE IS MY GREATEST GIFT

If I wasn't a writer…

The words left unwritten would charge erratically in my head and converse over my thoughts / my emotions would be stowed away in bags dusted by time as I wouldn't know how to unpack them / the world would seem ordinary, as it would no longer be my poem awaiting a romanticised life through my pen / the sunrise would be just the sun rising, and not an empowering poem with butternut colours of dawn caressing the page / the first fall of snow would simply be the weather, and not a glittering piece of prose / my wounds would be left exposed as no poetic words would have stitched them together / where would the lyrics go that overflow on pages of love notes for my soulmate?

If I wasn't a writer, if this passion didn't find me, I honestly don't know what I would do.

Libby Jenner

don't be shy, dearest butterfly

CLEANSE

Dew drop tears shower across my petal skin
and I open my arms for their embrace.
The rain cleanses my body,
and cuts through the ties
that burdens have knotted to me:
though staying soft on my skin
despite their daggering swipes.

And I weep,
a loud cry of bottled screams
whilst I walk in circles
under the weeping clouds,
so as not to have the puddles at my feet
freeze over
and leave me stuck in permanent picture
of my winter release.

Libby Jenner

don't be shy, dearest butterfly

WEATHERED BY CHANGE

Change is growth that is uncomfortable.

I want to hold in my breath, so I don't move the swollen clouds, because I am content in the weather I have adapted to. I don't know whether there is warmth from a pulsing sun or concocted storms beyond the wispy shield. But now the clouds are painted with grey and the droplets that cascade interrupt my regular broadcast.

Inevitable, it seems, for this phenomenon to linger. Sometimes waiting patiently to supply me with a new path to venture, other times restive and abrupt with its unannounced arrival.

No wonder change is so scary for those with an anxious heart: it is imperceptible. Overthinking cannot fathom an outcome, but instead give a reflection of your cavernous fears.

Though my heart is strung with nerves I take comfort in the thought that I have lived in thunderous storms, summer suns, lightning showers, guiding winds, freezing snows, and I am still breathing.

Though I am often weathered by change or eroded by its impact, I'd like to think that it wants to show me the unnoticed parts of my frame that were worn with fatigue, neglect, constraint, and need to be reformed: kindness may be its intent, even when the reality is cruel.

Libby Jenner

I want to hold my breath, so I don't move the swollen clouds.

Yet.

don't be shy, dearest butterfly

Libby Jenner

ICE ON WOUNDS

Tranquil thoughts,
like the delicate fall of snow,
caress me in streams.

Frost rimmed tributaries
barely overflowing with surges of pessimism,
anymore.

Cool…refreshing…rejuvenating…

I slide my feet into the water,
then let the ripples caress my thighs,
hug my torso,
brush my chest,
touch me all the way to my neck.
I lean back so that my hair swirls
like an icy lotus crown around me.

Calamities cannot follow me here,
so I breathe amongst the silence
that echoes around me
and let the water rinse me of pain.

Cool to turn my orange fires blue…. refreshing to quench my thirst for recreation…rejuvenating to awaken my intuition…

don't be shy, dearest butterfly

Libby Jenner

ANARCHIC AMBIENCE

Fresh green blades under frost
preserved in a resin of opalescent ice.
Ash rose dusk clouds powder the sky;
a crescent moon biting through.

Ignite *Ignite* *Ignite*

As silk winds brush my cheeks with snow
wise words from the woodlands,
sung as lullabies,
tuck themselves behind my ears.
And I run to the hearth I left ablaze.

Burn *Burn* *Burn*

Written on paper are my fears to destroy
and desires to incite.
The crackling fire of garnet sheen
wrote these words in dragon's breath smoke:

Burn it.
Burn them all.
Let my flames enshroud them to a crisp
and spit them out as ashes.

These, however,
Ignite them.
Let my flames worship them
and watch what blooms from their embers.

don't be shy, dearest butterfly

I open my eyes to a mango glow
and fumbling through the fire licked
logs of wood
a flower of phoenix hues
that is not burning,
but thriving.

Libby Jenner

don't be shy, dearest butterfly

YEAR FOUR

I am ready

The sky awaits, eclose

I am art

Crystal clear

Bestir myself to fly

Speaking to the river reflection

Shades of Autumnal change

Rebuilding my worth

Glowing

New avenues emerging

Pearl white paint, dry

Hopeful for what is to come

Libby Jenner

don't be shy, dearest butterfly

I AM READY

The peridot door spoke to me:
I heard its voice in a dream.
It told me it will open for me
and I must say goodbye to this home,
and the versions of me
that healed here,
because change is calling my name.

A smile tickled its way along my face.
And I pinched myself, just in case.
A dream this place has begun to feel,
and now I am ready
for something real.

Libby Jenner

don't be shy, dearest butterfly

THE SKY AWAITS

Don't be shy, dearest butterfly,
it's time to emerge from your ochre chrysalis.
Your ethereal journey is about to unfurl,
so, leap into the faint apricot skies
and leave your old home devoid of a miss.

You have outgrown the land
you so fondly grew in,
and your wings are hungry
for what awaits.
So fly, dearest butterfly,
amongst the amber light of dawn.

Let us see what stories
your transformed self
narrates.

Libby Jenner

don't be shy, dearest butterfly

I AM ART

If my life were an art piece
it would be painted with a vibrant tenacity,
or softened by elegant neutral hues.
I would like to see it change incessantly:
a new sculpture, print, or illustration,
so that I have a museum
overflowing with masterpieces
that display my ever-evolving existence.

Libby Jenner

don't be shy, dearest butterfly

CRYSTAL CLEAR

Under the stars of my jeweled thoughts
rest images of my future.
Crystal clear is my impending self
that my diamond manifestations made
unbreakable.

What a beautiful life will crystallise before me
because my sunstone soul embraced her worth.
After years of digging for an unknown discovery
my potential has, finally, been unearthed.

Libby Jenner

don't be shy, dearest butterfly

BESTIR MYSELF TO FLY

Chirping birds awake me,
upon drawing my curtains
I see their elegant frames
soaring in the milky mauve ether.

      I close my eyes tight and open them
          to see my house below me:
              a small figurine.
   Sheer heather hues swim in the forever
            stretching meadows.
      And light dipped paths meander
  amongst the viridian sea of grass.

  A catharsis of my deepest emotions
  drift through the feathers on my wings.
Ameliorating me from my suffered thoughts
  and leaving positivity to organise itself
      in the space that is pending
        an interior design.

I have come to learn that
I am more than a pretty existence:
more than a pretty bird in a cage
to be cooed at and praised
for my delicate fragility.
All would be complimentary
if not for the undertone that my vulnerability
makes me weak.

I am more than a pretty existence:
star infused galaxies rest in my wings

Libby Jenner

and each feathered strand of my being
is woven with each liberating choice I make.

This is an indefinite hiatus from a mindset
that shot arrows at my pennon.
And I intend to soar so high
that I can hear the universe's whispers
emitting from the stars.

>
> The existences of birds like me
> are beyond pretty:
> they are phenomenal.

don't be shy, dearest butterfly

Libby Jenner

SPEAKING TO THE RIVER REFLECTION

I hope you begin to fathom
how sunbeams hardly do justice
to the light you bring into our life.

In fact, the sun would kneel in awe
at our feet
if she saw how much
we radiate gold.

don't be shy, dearest butterfly

Libby Jenner

SHADES OF AUTUMNAL CHANGE

Maple leaves
change colour with the seasons.
Autumn entices them to smolder into
mesmerising shades of vermillion red.
Eventually, they leap gracefully to the ground,
a re-birth to fertilise the soil below.

Had you never

changed,

```
          n
       w
     o
   r
 g
```

bloomed,

```
f
  a
    l
      l
        e
          n
```

you would not be who you are today.

Like the maple leaves,

don't be shy, dearest butterfly

your leap of a fall
will help something grow.
And I hope whatever is nurtured
helps your character, mind, and soul.

Libby Jenner

don't be shy, dearest butterfly

REBUILDING MY WORTH

I combed the clouds,
and cracked sienna toned forests
into colour,
to reveal where the evil was at rest.
My voyage's intent was to dismantle
the tarnished parts of me
that were holding my power captive,
and embed them with a new enamel.

This process reminds me
that there is so much determination
in a strong woman,
who rebuilds herself when she breaks,
to anchor to moments
where her heart beats without rusting.

Libby Jenner

don't be shy, dearest butterfly

GLOWING

Embers of the day,
that were left burning into sundown,
frost the trees with an auburn glow.

Tenderly,
as if moulded with kind hands,
my own light begins to show.

Beams echo from my skin,
flowing over darkened bends.

A celebratory event for me, is necessary,
where past versions of myself can attend.

Libby Jenner

don't be shy, dearest butterfly

NEW AVENUES EMERGING

Creeping vines finally cut from my ankles,
this is the part where I walk away.

Today, I spit out:

Anxious constraints that
wrap my heart / words of
self-hatred that attack my
lungs / jealousy that
corrupts my thoughts /
anger that poisons my
behaviour

Now, I consume:

Kisses of the day that powder
me with adoration / honesty
garnished with kindness /
sunset caramels to compliment the
glow of my worth / love for my
passions that I once hid

Sprinkling flower seeds as I go,
I walk down a new avenue
that is named after me.
Or named after who it is
that will walk out from the other side.

Libby Jenner

don't be shy, dearest butterfly

PEARL WHITE PAINT, DRY

Icy violet salve on my broken skin
smoothing the parts that years of pain
had left coarse and unnurtured.
Curative, this winter has been
since I found a spec of white paint
on my wooden floor:
soaked into the board by my bed,
her bed,
our bed.

A vestigial flicker of my younger self.
How far, it is, she has come

Libby Jenner

don't be shy, dearest butterfly

HOPEFUL FOR WHAT IS TO COME

The next few days of this year
will be spent reflecting on all
that I have achieved.

And cutting the strings,
that negative habits,
knotted and tied to me.

I will not put pressure to set resolutions
and fall into the trap of
starting new.

Because I spent this year learning
to love myself
and accept all that wilted and grew.

I will try not to stray from opportunities
and to the peace in my life,
I will try to succumb.
For how incredible it would be
to further evolve
the incredible woman
I have become.

Libby Jenner

don't be shy, dearest butterfly

I AM
THE SUN AND MOON

Libby Jenner

don't be shy, dearest butterfly

I had just taken a nightly stroll under the eyes of the moon when the smell of burning wood twisted in the air around me, and I heard a faint cry from somewhere in the woods. Maybe the being in distress was looking for guidance in the same waning moon that was guiding me home? And maybe where I am seeking a light on my path, they need a light to find their way out of the dark, too, and back to themselves. I whispered the following words into the trees, and let the wind swoop them through breeze, in hope that whoever needed them would hear.

Libby Jenner

"Close your eyes and take in a breath,
let the moon-soaked earth beneath you
ground you in this moment.

Feel the moon and her light wash off
the stains that torrents of emotions
have carved into your thoughts.

On the breath that you release,
expel not just the unwanted air
but the unwanted energy,
and monotone ambitions,
that were treating your body as a host.

And repeat,
until there is nothing left in you
that is leaving your body breathless."

don't be shy, dearest butterfly

The following morning, I noticed that the greenhouse had been eaten away by the weather. With a bag of tools in tow, for repotting any plants that now would have smashed pots from the storm, I unlocked one of the double doors to the greenhouse and relaxed in its humidity. The scent of greenery instantly calming me. As I walked in, I noticed there was a smashed window, so I began picking up the shards and I put them into a nearby ceramic pot I had been storing flower seeds in (the seeds I placed in the large pockets of my dungarees for safe keeping). Seeing the greenhouse window shattered in a precarious mess got me thinking about my own fragility: how easy it is for my walls to break and for my sensitivity to overwhelm me. Which, combined, leaves me in broken pieces much like the green house window.

But I don't perceive that as a negative trait. For there is so much strength in my vulnerability: it has allowed me to be passionate, kind, empathetic, and understanding. And these are the traits that guide my morals, lead me to amazing people, and help teach me how to accept all that I am.

Libby Jenner

I *am* fragile like glass.

But glass is most dangerous
when broken.
And it's also more beautiful
when in fragmented parts.

So, if I break,
I remember the strength
in my broken shards,
and the splendour
of the scattered rainbows
when the sun strikes them.

I am powerful
even when I am fragile,

I am beautiful
even when I am in pieces.

don't be shy, dearest butterfly

There are only so many sizes of pots for a plant to grow in before the roots crave more soil; there are only so many extensions of greenhouse walls and ceilings you can build before the branches hunch over and groan, there is only so much you can do (and with what you are given) before you must move into an environment where you can grow more.

I have lived in this wonderful place for many years, and each season a new pot served me more space to explore myself. Now, however, what I need is to be unconfined. I want to have roots stretching miles long and leaves basking up into the clouds with vines crawling in every direction.

I cannot flourish here, anymore, and although I seek so much comfort in this home I have created, I am ready for more.

I accept the uncertainty: my fear of change has cloaked my vision for too long.

Libby Jenner

Trapped behind

a glass wall.
Freedom printed
on my eggshell skin,
how fitting.
My purpose
barely fulfilled:
I'm devoid of
floral company.
Where I wish to be
is in the centre of a table
sunlight

P
  O
    U
      R
        I
          N
            G

over me
and the flowers I hold
beaming in her warmth.

Slowly,
I will edge
closer
to the ledge
until
suddenly

 I fall
Smash

don't be shy, dearest butterfly

and I, a pile of scattered eggshells,
will slowly shut my eyes,
as water   o o z e s   around me,
and the flowers rest
in pieces at my grave.

My last sight being
the painted butterflies soaring
into the wondrous sky through an open window.

Finally, free.

Libby Jenner

After fixing the greenhouse, I ran indoors to pack my rucksack with memories and monuments of my time in my home.

Shards of the greenhouse glass wrapped in a sand coloured cloth / An old notepad of past writings that I used to keep in my jacket pocket before I came to the garden / a sunflower surrounded by a colourful array of smaller flowers which I pressed into a glass frame / my favourite collection of books about fantasy tales and elegant poetry that are bound by years of adoration, and have love pressed into each tattered page / a tiny draw string bag with flower seeds inside, so I can take flowers from my garden to my new home / rose petals that I dried in the sun / a clipping of the monstera that I can propagate / a handful of pens / and lastly, the book that the guide gave me.

I found another notebook identical to mine on my bookshelf a few months ago, but I didn't have room for it in my bulging rucksack, so I left it on the small table next to my plush peacock chair.

don't be shy, dearest butterfly

When I dared to be bold
I learnt that it doesn't mean
I can't be gentle, exposed, or kind:
it means I am all those things,
not as a service to others,
but as an investment in myself.

Libby Jenner

The trees had already started wavering as I whispered my goodbyes. The yellow of the sunflowers didn't look so bright to me, anymore. It wasn't as though the enchantment was fading but I knew I had to leave, and my garden was helping me do that. But the illusion had not fully disappeared, because now I harness the magic that filled this garden with hope: and every cell in my body is diffusing the glitter of its enchanting nature into my veins.

Now, in my new home, I can bring the ethereal environment with me. And I am so excited to test the thresholds of my power in a place that won't restrict my potential.

don't be shy, dearest butterfly

Your heart is fragile, no?

Take it, go on,
reach beneath your ribcage
and place it in the flames
that blaze vermillion and gold.
Look in the hearth,
that's it, beneath the embers
what's there, hm?

I don't understand, how is it still beating?

You have been told that your fire
is to be feared,
that your ferocity
is untamed and dangerous,
that your behaviour
breaks things around you.
But, darling, you are magic
and your flames need nothing
if not constant kindling.

Women are magic:
a mess of black flames, rose gold bones,
and witch blood in our veins.
We spin worlds off their axis
as a simple procrastination game.

Skin sewn by threads of stars,
portals concealed in our eyes,
celestial whispers woven into our hair:
the living form of a poet's design.

Listen to the wildflower's gossip,
as they bathe in our pools of light.

Libby Jenner

See how they sing of women in spring
whose fingertips trickle magic at night.

*(what the blossom tree spoke to me when I said
goodbye)*

don't be shy, dearest butterfly

For the last time, I decided to bask in the beautiful life I have had in this garden of recovery and thank this home that nurtured me, and I nurtured in return.

I knew that when I walked to the door in the woods it would open.

It was time to go.

Libby Jenner

Bold strokes of gold-washed skies
dusted my vision as I looked up into the clouds.

I took a moment away from pruning
the white roses in my garden,
how beautiful they are in bloom,
to let the edges of the sun caress
my glowing skin.

I smiled, with the beauty only comparable
to dawn kissing dusk,
and sighed as the healing thoughts
flowed through the cool waves of my mind.

Shades of hurt are now replaced
with positive intentions,
harsh anxiety traded for confident cues,
and past wounds now hemmed with caring strings.

I am proud of the person I am,
and I became her
by watering the white roses
that I already had.
Rather than hurting myself
to paint the petals red.

I have bloomed in ways
not even my dreams
could have prepared me for.
All because I tended to my own roses,
first.

don't be shy, dearest butterfly

I was just about to start walking into the woods of my new story when a slight breeze hit the back of my neck, and I turned to see a wooden door appear in the middle of my garden.

Libby Jenner

I walked, curiously, towards it. Familiarity tickling at my thoughts but no memory surfacing, yet.

don't be shy, dearest butterfly

I twisted the door handle and let the light trickle over me and into the room that the door opened into.

Libby Jenner

The light illuminated a bewildered child with misty blue eyes in the middle of a grey room, next to a pearl white canvas.

don't be shy, dearest butterfly

I couldn't help but stand in a stunned silence as her features became recognisable to me.

Libby Jenner

She couldn't see my face, but tears were streaming down my complexion.

don't be shy, dearest butterfly

I took a deep breath, composed my voice, and said:

Libby Jenner

"Hey, I am your guide, would you like to take a walk with me?"

don't be shy, dearest butterfly

Libby Jenner

ACKNOWLEDGMENTS

To begin, thank you for reading my book. You are an incredible being, and I am so grateful that you chose to read my words. Please remind yourself that you are wonderful when wilting and blooming, when miserable and when encouraged: you are a beautiful balance.

Thank you to my phenomenal best friend, Annabelle, who has believed in me since we were children, who has never second-guessed my abilities, and who has shown me a love so pure and unfaltering. Annabelle, it has, and will continue to be, an honour that I have witnessed you bloom into the incredible woman that you are. The love I have for you is in a never-ending abundance. And thank you for designing such a beautiful cover for this book, I am in awe of your talent, and I am so proud of you.

Thank you to my incredible family for supporting me on my journey as a writer, and as a person in general. Thank you to my sisters: growing up with you and watching you all thrive and continue to do so has been and will be an extraordinary adventure. Thank you to my mum for teaching me what it is to be emotional and complex, and that it is okay to be that way. I love all of you immensely.

Thank you to the love of my life, my gorgeous, for inspiring me with your creativity, determined mindset, and kindness. Being with you is like being showered in sunlight, and not a day goes by where I don't smile at how in love I am, with you. Thank you

don't be shy, dearest butterfly

for unconditionally loving me, supporting me, and being my personal dose of heaven. I love you endlessly, and always.

Thank you to my friends that have listened to me chatter about this book for goodness knows how long yet still got excited with me at all my writing milestones: thank you for believing in me and loving me when I was that little girl by a canvas. I appreciate all of you: you each have a slice of my heart that is filled with adoration for you.

Thank you to my fellow writers in the Instagram writing community. Your words always leave me in awe: you are inspirations. I am so grateful for your encouraging words and spurring nature. Without you, I would not have as much confidence as I do now to write this book!

Lastly, I would like to make thanks to myself. Thank you, me, for believing in my abilities and never giving up. Thank you for choosing your passion incessantly and following your poetic heart, because this dream- like reality where I can publish my words for people to read is one which I hope to never wake from. I am grateful that my words are now so gentle, and I am so proud of my strength and creativity that binds this book together. I am incredible.

Libby Jenner

don't be shy, dearest butterfly

ABOUT THE AUTHOR

Libby is a 21-year-old English poet studying Creative Writing at University. Libby began writing and reading poetry in secondary school as a therapeutic outlet when she began struggling with her mental health. Since believing in the potential of her creativity, she now writes with the intention to inspire readers with her words and create a safe space for them to heal.

Don't be shy, dearest butterfly is Libby's debut book, and will be on bookshelves amongst many of her stunning creations that are yet to come.

You can join Libby's poetry community on her Instagram account @libbyjenner.poetry

don't be shy, dearest butterfly

Printed in Great Britain
by Amazon